JUST ADD NOTHING

Salvation is by Grace Alone,
But do You Believe it?

✧ ✧ ✧

by
Gary L Johnson

Copyright © 2007 by Gary L. Johnson

Just Add Nothing
by Gary L. Johnson

Printed in the United States of America

ISBN 978-1-60266-534-7

All rights reserved solely by the author. The author guarantees all contents are original and do not infringe upon the legal rights of any other person or work. No part of this book may be reproduced in any form without the permission of the author. The views expressed in this book are not necessarily those of the publisher.

Unless otherwise indicated, Bible quotations are taken from *Concordia Self-Study Bible,* New International Version of the Bible. Copyright © 1986 by Concordia Publishing House, St. Louis, MO

www.xulonpress.com

PREFACE

✣ ✣ ✣

Greetings. If you are reading this book, may God Bless you. It may well be that He has led you to do so. As you read, I hope my work, if nothing else, will bring you to a closer knowledge of your eternal future with the Lord Jesus.

We all have to be on the same page, so to speak, as you read forward and I want you to know what my statement of faith is:

First, I will hope you have heard of Jesus Christ and know that He is God.

Second, there is no other God but God… The Father, the Son – Jesus Christ, and the Holy Spirit. Nothing else and no other deity worshiped by others on this planet is that same

God. There is none other God than the one true Lord – three in one.

Third, there is no way to salvation except through Jesus Christ.

Fourth, the Bible, 66 books as it exists today, is the complete Word of God; inspired by Him and written by Him through those who authored the letters. Also, that those works and letters were not influenced in any way that God did not intend for them to be influenced by the personal attributes and opinions of the ones writing them.

Fifth, God knows everything and is all-powerful. This is my belief and everything in this book springs from that foundation.

Finally, let me say that I am not professing taking Grace for granted! My book deals with an emotional subject. The effort here is to strip down this wonderful gift – salvation – to it's most simple level. Salvation should bring about a change in us, however, this is a subject for a book all in it's own.

Praise God for His way to eternal life with Him!

✣ ✣ ✣

I want to offer special thanks to Pastor David Schultz who was a sounding board during the writing of my book. Also, though he may never know how much, I am especially grateful to Pastor Eugene Heckmann for doggedly sticking to his guns and teaching scriptural truth. Pastor Heckmann baptized me, confirmed me, participated our wedding and baptized our children. He later remarried both of my parents. Other than my dad and my Grandmother Sadie, few have had a greater impact on my life. Mom and dad – thanks for making the decision to take us to Church and for having us baptized !

FOR

✥ ✥ ✥

Diane, Joseph and Michael.
You are God's true Blessing in my life !

INTRODUCTION

✤ ✤ ✤

I am a layman and, except for some training in the LCMS as a Pastoral Assistant, have no formal education within the Church. However, it is easy to forget that as a mature Christian, we have the ability and the obligation to share what we know with others of the faith. I've had the benefit of studying the Bible for thirty odd years now under some very learned pastors and believe I have a very clear understanding of our personal salvation if we strip away denominational baggage. In the following chapters, where the Bible is quoted, it is from the Concordia Self-Study Bible, New International Version. Where it might add clarity, I include the study notes directly after a quoted verse in parenthesis. Although I've started many times to write this book, I could never get comfortable with exactly what form it might take or how I might present the subject. Finally, I believe the Lord got tired of waiting on me and began to urge, with ever stronger means, that I just get going and trust Him.

Am I really saved? I would bet that most Christians have asked themselves this question at some point in their life. Maybe you've asked yourself this question recently. The question, in and of itself, doesn't make us bad. Instead, I believe, it shows a belief that there is a God of this creation and we really want to know where we stand with him. How we ask the question is important. The question is not, and never can be, are **we** saved. God made salvation available for all mankind and so it's easy to look at the issue in whole-world terms. The issue is *totally* singular and personal for each living soul. Am "I" saved – that's the question. The Bible is certainly the resource for knowing but, for me anyway, hasn't always been that clear in the way it presents the answer. Neither, for my part, have the professional clergy of our time answered this question with certainty. Man has created many 'denominations' flying under the overall flag of Christianity. Like any making of man, they are imperfect and they have made the answer to this simple and all-important question – less than clear for many Christians.

Christ said in Matthew 11:28-30 *"Come to me, all you who are weary and burdened, and I will give you rest. Take my yoke upon you and learn from me, for I am gentle and humble in heart, and you will find rest for your souls. <u>For my yoke is easy and my burden is light.</u>"* Emphasis added.

Memorize these words and remember them while you read this book because there are things which have become very important to church denominations – and men – which were of minor concern to our Savior in terms of our salvation. He and His disciples preached a message of salvation which was clear and precise. A pastor of our Church once said to me, "We often confuse the words in the 'books' of the Gospel with - the Gospel message." He explained in a separate communication later that a proper distinction between Law and Gospel requires more than an assumption that the Gospels are all Gospel. There is plenty of Law in the Gospels and there is plenty of Gospel and God's grace revealed in the Old Testament as well. This 'confusion' is at the root of our wonderings about our personal salvation. If you get nothing else from reading this work, I hope you can once and for all answer this very personal question with inner conviction and assurance. May God bless you as you ponder the most important question you might ever ask yourself -- Am I really saved?

TABLE OF CONTENTS

✜ ✜ ✜

The Bible Says 17
The Paradox 27
The Great Need 39
The Requirement 45
The Way 57
Baptism 63
What About Specific Sins? 71
That Grace Thing – It's a Big Thing 81
Judgment and Reward vs. Salvation 95
The Question – The Answer 103

THE BIBLE SAYS

✣ ✣ ✣

Corinthians 2:13

"This is what we speak, not in words taught us by human wisdom but in words taught by the Spirit."

✣ ✣ ✣

The Bible, the 66 books which we have bound together for our use today, are ancient writings. They are inspired – written – by God. We'll get into this however I wanted to first bring up the subject of how we should interpret scripture. There are three ways in which scripture can be read and interpreted:

1) Allegorically
2) Historical Grammatical
3) Historical Critical

Many in our contemporary time would like to use method number one. They believe that the Bible is a book of symbolic stories, or allegories, only. As such, they are free to decide what those 'stories' mean to them. They can assign whatever weight they feel comfortable with at any given time or no weight at all if things get a little too uncomfortable. Others like method three. They accept that the Bible is historical in nature and literal in it's representation of time, people and events. However, they critically interpret it's meanings based on human understanding and their own presuppositions and assumptions. In other words – man decides what God meant to say. Edward W.A. Koehler made this point in his writings:

> *It is not our business to sit in judgment on what we have learned to be the plain sense of the Bible text, accepting what agrees, and rejecting what does not agree with our personal views and rationalizations. This 'judicial' or 'critical' use of human reason is absolutely out of place with respect to divine truths. Where God has spoken, the right of private judgment ceases. We must, therefore, not 'correct' the Scriptures according to our ideas and logical deductions, but we must correct our thoughts and ideas according to the Scriptures.* [1]

Since God directed the writings of the Bible Himself and since He is very capable of saying what He wants to say – the only true way to read and interpret the Bible is the second method. Method 2, Historical Grammatical, accepts that the Bible is factual and historical in nature and 'grammatically' lets scripture interpret scripture. When we read the text of the Bible we are to let other verses in other books and chapters support and cross reference it's meanings. The Bible does this very well. As we read, and if we're watching for it to happen, we will run across verses which allude to or directly reference sayings, promises, covenants, etc., which are in other verses in other books of the Bible. Scripture interprets scripture. More than that, scripture validates scripture. By sticking with this method of reading the Bible, we take out the possibility of our desires, emotions, lack of knowledge and biases clouding the intended lessons from God. We lessen the tendency to make His words say more – or less – than He meant them to say.

How did we end up with the 66 books of the Bible and how do we know that the books included are authentic? God says, in the Bible, that His words are, in fact, His words. In Luke 24:27,44; John 5:39; and Hebrews 10:7, Jesus says that what was written about him in the Old Testament would come to pass. Romans 3:2 and Hebrews 5:12 refer to the Old Testament as the Word of God. In 1 Corinthians 2:13 we read, *"This is what we speak, not in words taught us by human wisdom but in words taught by the Spirit."* In Paul's second letter to the Thessalonians 2:13, when referring to what he had written to them earlier he says, *"...you accepted it not as the word of men, but as it actually is, the Word of God."* Saint Peter writes in 2 Peter 3:15-16 of the inspiration of St. Paul, *"...Paul also wrote to you with the wisdom that God gave him. He writes the same way in all his letters..."*

Earlier, in 2 Peter 1:21, Peter writes, *"For prophecy never had its origin in the will of man, but men spoke from God as they were carried along* [moved] *by the Holy Spirit."* Another good example is in Revelation 22:18,19, *"...if anyone adds anything to them, God will add to him the plagues described in this book. And if anyone takes words away from this book of prophecy, God will take away from him his share in the tree of life..."*

There are many other references in New and Old Testament writings which state that words in the Bible are specifically those of the Lord God himself and none other than He. In the book, *Evidence That Demands a Verdict*, author Charles Wesley writes:

The Bible must be the invention either of good men or angels, bad men or devils, or of God. However, it was not written by good men, because good men would not tell lies by saying 'Thus saith the Lord;' it was not written by bad men because they would not write about doing good duty, while condemning sin, and themselves to hell; thus, it must be written by divine inspiration. [2]

There is a great web site at www.AllAboutTruth.org. The articles published there deal specifically with Bible origin and authenticity. I would like to quote a paragraph from that site which states very nicely how the Bible can stand on it's own against other books and even ancient literature:

> God does not leave us with just claims of His divine handiwork in the Bible, but also supports it with compelling evidence. The design of the Bible itself is a miracle. Written over more than 1,500 years by vastly different writers, yet every book in the Bible is consistent in its message. These 66 books talk about history, prophecy, poetry, and theology. Despite their complexity, differences in writing styles and vast time periods, the books of the Bible agree miraculously well in theme, facts and cross-referencing. No human beings could have planned such an intricate combination of books over a 1,500-year time span. Bible manuscripts (remember there were no printing presses until 1455) have survived despite weather, persecution and time. Most ancient writings written on weak materials like papyrus have vanished all together. Yet many copies of the Old Testament scriptures survived. For instance, the Dead Sea Scrolls contain all books of the Old Testament, except Ester, and have been dated to before the time of Christ. Consider Julius Caesar's "Gallic Wars." Only ten copies written about 1,000 years after the event are in existence. In comparison, there are over 24,000+

New Testament manuscripts, the earliest one dating to within 24 years after Christ. [3]

The Old Testament scriptures were brought forward in history by the Jews and early believers and by their consistent honor of the writings, those manuscripts are accepted as authentic and correct. The New Testament has come under attack because "men" decided which of the 27 books assembled were to be included – canonized. Again, the Bible itself takes the lead in this fight. 2 Peter 3:16 seems to take for granted that Paul's letters were already considered inspired scripture just like the Old Testament. 1 Timothy 5:18 joins an Old Testament reference and a new Testament reference and calls them both scripture. [4] The Bible, 66 books as we have it from God, was canonized through consistent use of men in their study over hundreds of years. Consistent use is what has canonized – chosen – the books of the Bible. Early church fathers studied long over every text available. Every text was compared in context and meaning, use and language, to every other. The slightest error or miss-statement led to that manuscript being considered - held out - such that those remaining are, and were prayerfully considered, the ones which God would have us hold as His complete Word. An example of the timeline under which these books were scrutinized is as follows:

The Codex Barococcio, 206 AD, includes 64 of the 66 books of today's Bible except Ester and Revelation. Those were already declared inspired by Justin, Martyr, Irenaeus, Clement, Tertullian and the Muratorian Cannon. [5]

In 230 AD, Origen declared that all Christians acknowledged as scripture the four Gospels, Acts, the epistles of Paul, 1 Peter, 1 John and Revelation. [6]

Early 300's AD, all new Testament books were being used in the mainstream Church body. [7]

367 AD, Athanasius formally circulated the Easter Letter that listed all 27 books as canonical. In 393 AD, the Synod of Hippo also recognized all 27 books as canonical. In addition, the church fathers, Jerome (340-420 AD) and Augustine (354-430 AD) published their lists of 27 books completing the New Testament. [8]

The Bible can be trusted. The English translation, the King James version, is an exhaustive translation and widely used by Christian scholars as a base translation of the original texts. The New International Version and Revised Standard Edition are just as exhaustive in their attempt to hold every nuance of the King James translation but in language which is more understandable in the 21st century. Any of these three translations will not lead you intentionally astray in your search for Biblical Truth. The key thing to remember is to let the Bible interpret itself – by cross reference – in areas where you may have questions as to the meanings of any given verse. Each of the translations has footnotes and reference marks which lead us to other verses which define or support that particular verse. God gave His Word for all mankind. It's a cinch that not all of us would be Bible scholars with Ph.D. behind our name. We shouldn't need to be. While the details might, at times, get deep or a bit confusing – the overall message is always clear and always points towards Christ Jesus as the way to salvation.

THE PARADOX

✣ ✣ ✣

John 6:44 – Jesus is speaking

"No one can come to me unless the Father who sent me draws him, and I will raise him up at the last day."

✣ ✣ ✣

Free will. God gave it to man and only man at creation. Free will is a powerful fact of our relationship with the Almighty and is woefully misunderstood by most Christians. Ponder this thought:

<u>We can decide to deny Christ but we cannot decide to accept Him.</u>

Read those words again and think them over a bit. Scripture tells us that we, by our own power or decision, cannot come to Christ. From the very beginning, we have nothing at all to do with our own salvation. Several verses speak directly to this truth in scripture.

John 6:44 – *Jesus is speaking "No one can come to me unless the Father who sent me draws him, and I will raise him up at the last day." (Note: 6:44 draws-*

people do not come to Christ on their own initiative; the Father draws them.)

1 Cor. 12:3 *"Therefore I tell you that no one who is speaking by the Spirit of God says, 'Jesus be cursed', and no one can say, 'Jesus is Lord,' except by the Holy Spirit."*

Eph. 2:8,9 *"For it is by Grace you have been saved, through faith – and this not from yourselves, it is the gift of God – not by works, so that no one can boast."*

There is no such thing as a 'decision' to be saved. You and I cannot declare that we are saved and make it so. If we know so and believe it – we certainly should declare it! But walking up to the front of the church or shouting those words in some form from the hilltop doesn't accomplish a thing. More than this, it is not our decision at all. Christ saved us. We'll look at what He did to accomplish our salvation later but, for now, Christ – saved *us* — is the simple fact we all need to know and keep in mind. His work of salvation, available for all mankind, is a fact and there is nothing any man can do to change it. It's done – it's over – it's finished – salvation is won. Nothing, and no one ever created, can take this gift away from any person born since the resurrection or yet to be born. The paradox – do you believe it….While we have no power to accept Christ, He gives us the freedom not to believe in Him once He makes Himself known to us.

Think about that word – believe. What do you really believe? Notice, the question was not what do you really *think*. Belief is not an easy thing to describe because it's personal from one person to another. Maybe the best example would be our belief that we will take that next breath or that there will be daylight when we wake up tomorrow morning. We trust these things will happen. So much so, that we don't really give them a thought from one day to the next. Even further to the idea is we *know* that the Lord could stop either from happening, and will at a time of His choosing. However, we constantly take for granted that His time won't be today – or even tomorrow. We consider the weather or happenings of the coming day but not that the day – itself – will exist. We simply 'know' that there will be a day. That feeling, if you will, is as close as I can come to describing the concept of belief. Stop right now and think it through. Think of some things that you really believe. Grasp the feeling in your mind when you think of those things. Get a handle on it because that little nuance is very important when speaking or thinking of your salvation.

The oddity of this thing – belief – is that there is no attachment to *how we feel* at any given moment. We might wakeup with the worst case of flu in history but don't consider whether the sun will rise. One might win the lottery, become an instant multi-millionaire and not once consider that the Lord might stop our next breath from happening. Feelings have nothing to do with belief. The point I am getting to is simply this; how we feel about Jesus, or even God in general, at any given moment or period in our life doesn't really have anything at all to do with our belief in Jesus – or what he did for us. At one moment, I may not feel happy at all. But, overall and if asked, I would say that I am a happy person. Overall, I'm happy. The fact that there are hours or maybe days when I don't *feel* happy doesn't change the fact that, generally, I have been and am happy.

It's safe to say that we take our beliefs for granted. Yes, but, we know in the back of our mind that we are free to not believe these things. We could, I suppose, convince ourselves that we are really about to die, or know it to be a fact. One might believe that the world is about to end at any second. The point is, once the seed is planted, we develop and determine our beliefs. It takes time, the Holy Spirit, example, persistence – and willingness - to form a belief or else an undisputable set of facts. Our beliefs are our own and contained wholly within our being and they are slightly different for each one of us. God, at creation, gave each of us the freedom and ability to change or deny our own beliefs. Free will.

So, now that we have a handle on the concept of belief, let's move on to the next part of the paradox. Free will. Free will vs. salvation. In the beginning, there was the law. A system of rules and consequences set out by the Lord himself as a result of the fall into sin in the Garden of Eden. This – law – was what guided early believers and determined what would happen when they faced God in judgment. I write in passed-tense here because the law, in regard to how we – present day - are saved, no longer exists. However, the law could not save – it could only condemn. Through Christ Jesus, Christian believers have been freed from the chains of the law.

Rom. 8:1,2 *"Therefore, there is now no condemnation for those who are in Christ Jesus, because through Christ Jesus the law of the Spirit of Life set me free from the law of sin and death." (Note: 8:1 condemnation- The law brings condemnation because it points out, stimulates and condemns sin. But the Christian is no longer 'under law' [vs. 6:14])*

Rom. 6:14 *"For sin shall not be your master, because you are not under law, but under grace." (Note: 6:14: not under law- The meaning is not that the Christian has been freed from all moral authority [responsibility]. He has, however, been freed from the law in the manner in which God's people were under the law in the OT era.")*

Remember the apostle Paul in his letter to the Romans. In that text, Paul recounts the total helplessness of the human condition and position in our relationship to the law. We sin. We *are* sin and therein lie's the problem. We cannot help but to sin – everyday – every week – throughout our whole life. The Lord knew this and knew that He had to allow for a method for us to achieve perfection – in His eyes. The law required payment – restitution if you will – for sin. This 'payment' we could not produce or procure on our own and, so, early Christians were required to bring living animal sacrifices to the altar in atonement for their sins.. Our default in payment (inability to pay) meant that our souls were sentenced to serve out eternity in hell. God did not want this for His children. A Perfect Being and not having the desire to tolerate imperfection, God devised a perfect plan for the salvation of humanity to take the place of the law. There had to be a 'perfect' payment ***once and for all*** which would satisfy the requirement of the law and a perfect God. A one-time atonement and payment which nobody created by God could alter, add to, subtract from, or modify. That payment came in the form of the death and resurrection of our Savior, Jesus Christ. There could be no other way. In the text of each of the Gospel books, Matthew through John, there is the recount of Jesus' final words – "it is finished." Remember those words as you read the following chapters. Those three words are possibly some of the most important ones for Christians to memorize and recall. Take hold of them and own them. Humanity could never live up to the perfection required by the law. God gave us the miracle gift of perfection in His son Jesus Christ that all humankind might be saved.

> John 3:16-18 - *Jesus is speaking "For God so loved the world that he gave his one and only Son, that whoever believes in him shall not perish but have eternal life. For God did not send his Son into the world to condemn the world, but to save the world through him. Whoever believes in him is not condemned, but whoever does not believe stands condemned already because he has not believed in the name of God's one and only Son." (Note: 3:18 believes...does not believe- not speaking of momentary beliefs and doubts but of continuing, settled faith.)*

The ultimate paradox... We are free not to believe in the one who has saved us – Jesus. We have nothing at all to do with the fact that He did save us and, more that this, our salvation can only be received from Him as a gift. We don't determine if we will receive the gift – God has. Again, we do not 'decide' to be saved. This can only happen in conjunction with and by the power of the Holy Spirit.

By our own power, we cannot accept Jesus. However, once we hear the Truth, with our free will, we can deny it. Think of "free will" as an ATM bank card for a moment from the Intergalactic Bank of Faith. A bank card which is totally and singularly yours, which will work for nobody else and which nobody else can use even if they steal it. In fact, there is no way for it to be stolen. This very special bank card was given to you when you were born, you didn't ask for it and you didn't have a choice of whether you wanted it or not. You are a creation of God and He gave it to you just like He has given this special card to every person who was, has been, or will be, born. We get possession of the bank card when we are baptized or come to faith. So, it is a very restricted bank card indeed. When you were baptized, God placed a Billion Dollars worth of Faith into your special ATM account. Remember, from the moment of your baptism, no matter what age it occurs, you have total use and control of this special ATM account. The other odd thing about this particular account is the fact that we cannot make any deposits. God makes all the deposits from His Love and Grace. There is nothing you or I can do, no action, no work, which can add to that account in any way.

God is an unusual sort of banker. He loves to have people withdraw from their ATM accounts. In fact, as we withdraw from the account, He adds faith dollars back in so that the amount of faith available to us is always a billion dollars worth. However, God starts to get worried when the account becomes inactive. When there are no withdrawals, it signifies to Him that we feel we are getting by fine without His salvation dollars. God, Himself, will never – ever – close a faith account. He keeps the account open as long as we will allow Him to. However, just like with our worldly bank cards, etc., **we** have the ability to close the account. We'll talk about this more in the chapter on Grace but for now, think of "free will" as our ability to actually close our special ATM faith account. In order to close the account, we have to knowingly press the "NO" button for the question which asks: "Do you believe that there is a God and that He sent his Son, Jesus, to save you?" The choice is Yes or No. If we choose no – then – we have closed our ATM account with God. We close it, not him.

Once believers begin to use their account, I believe it is really rare for them to actually close it. However, the Bible tells us that it does and can happen. We can't open the account or make any deposits into it – but we can close it because God gives us the total ownership over it. Free Will.

THE GREAT NEED

✥ ✥ ✥

Romans 5:12

"Therefore, just as sin entered the world through one man, and death through sin, and in this way death came to all men, because all sinned."

✢ ✢ ✢

Why do I need to be saved? What does it mean – to me – to *be saved*? Remember back to Genesis. God created us and everything else – in six, 24 hour, days. At the end of His work He made the comment – "…it was very good." In Godly terms, "good" means devoid of ***anything*** bad. He created man and then woman as a partner for man. God sent the new couple into a wonderful, beautiful, perfect garden and gave it to them to keep and live in - happily ever after. There was no death. There was no decay. There was no sickness. Death entered into the picture at the moment Adam took a bite of the forbidden fruit. (I believe this shoots down the possibility that God's six "days" of creation were really thousands or millions of years and not a 24 hour day. If that were so and if things were 'evolving' during His creation then there would have needed to be death and decay for that process to work. The Bible strictly says that none of that – at all – existed prior to the fall of man.)

Right here I need to diverge a bit. The Bible tells of the fall of Lucifer (Satan). Lucifer was an angle and he challenged God in Heaven. He, Lucifer, was a *creation* of God. This is a paramount fact and one we tend to let pass. Lucifer was not and - is not – a god. He has only power and ability *allowed* by God and for a specific period of time – known only to God. When Lucifer and his followers got thrown out of Heaven, his angel followers were sent to hell and he, Lucifer, was allowed to be loose on the earth. This, in itself, did not harm man in his relationship with God. Man, at this point, was still perfect and without sin in the beautiful Garden of Eden. Apparently, Lucifer carries a grudge, or maybe misery loves company, because he took his first opportunity to get back at God by trying to pollute God's perfect creation on earth. I say 'trying' because Lucifer could not do this wicked thing on his own – he needed man to go along with the deal.

As a result of the great sin of Adam in the garden, we, everyone ever born since that moment, were forever tarnished in the eyes of the Lord God. Fast forward to today and this means that you and I have a great need as a result of that great sin. St. Paul tells us about sin and the result of what happened in the garden:

Rom 5:12 *"Therefore, just as sin entered the world through one man, and death through sin, and in this way death came to all men, because all sinned."*

Every day, you and I sin. Whether it is the angry word or gesture at the driver who just made us mad or that time we spend on the internet at work instead of doing our job – we all sin. Just one of those sins, ever, is enough to make us imperfect and in immediate need of forgiveness. Without that forgiveness, we would be doomed to an eternity in hell. God has spoken many times in the Bible about this fact. Even more, He has let us know how willing He is to forgive our sins.

As time progressed, however, it became evident that there had to be a better way. There needed to be a way to save us from ourselves. This 'way' had to be forever active, available for every person created, and totally fulfilling of the need. This new method to attain 'perfection' in God's eyes had to be a thing that was forever enough and never needed anything else added to it by anyone. Sinning is when we do something wrong and, unfortunately, I still do – every day. So, you and I have this need because we sin.

Through Christ, we can become "new." But how can I be new if I'm still me? There is a verse in 2 Corinthians which has always been particularly confusing to me. Paul tells us that once we have Christ, we are a new creation.

> 2 Cor. 5:17 *"Therefore, if anyone is in Christ, he is a new creation; the old has gone, the new has come!"*

(Note: new creation- Redemption is the restoration and fulfillment of God's purposes in creation and this takes place in Christ, through whom all things were made and in whom all things are restored or created anew.)

There are many days when I don't feel new at all and my sinful nature has a very strong hold on me. After some thought and research, I believe that this verse, and others similar to it, have a different meaning than that of a new physical creation – which is how many people read it. In fact, once we have Christ – in the Father's eyes – we are a **totally** new creation. This has to be it. He *sees* us as the new creation we are through and because of Grace. Our sinful nature is still certainly with us – but not in His eyes. He sees a Saint. So if, like me, you have ever read that verse and felt like something didn't make sense take heart. You're not alone and there's nothing wrong. We have to remember all the promises of the New Testament when we are reading small sections of the separate books which compose it. We have to consider the context of the words relative to the promise we have from God. All His promises are in the light of Grace and made to believers who, in His loving eyes, are made perfect through Christ Jesus. Despite of what we see in ourselves – He sees us as new.

THE REQUIREMENT

✥ ✥ ✥

Romans 3:10-12

"As it is written: There is no one righteous, not even one; there is no one who understands, no one who seeks God. All have turned away, they have together become worthless; there is no one who does good, not even one"

✥ ✥ ✥

There was a particularly dark time in my Christian life not too long ago. Diane and I had been married for about 10 years and had two boys. Michael, the youngest, was 14 months old at the time. Diane and I were happy in every way together. We lived just blocks from parents and our church and in a home we dearly loved. It was small but we had worked together to spruce it up and would have been satisfied to stay there for a long while.

Living across the street from us was a family with a 28 year old son who had a severe mental illness. One morning, I decided to take our youngest son out and go for a walk. It was a really beautiful, crisp, morning. One of those that the Lord gives us every so often which make you thankful to be alive. That guy across the street, the son, was a menace. Mental illness is a terrible disease. He heard voices and was certain that I wanted to date his girlfriend - who didn't exist. He had followed friends leaving our home, screamed obscenities at us when we were in our front yard and shot his shotgun over our heads one morning as we returned from church. He loudly and openly threatened to kill me on several occasions. I began to hate this man who seemed intent on doing real harm to me or my wife and children. As much as we loved being so close to our parents and our church – we knew we had to move. I didn't want to kill him. One morning as I put the .38 snub nose revolver in my jeans pocket I remember thinking that thought. "Thou shall not kill" ran through my mind, as it had many times in recent weeks. The sun was bright in the morning sky and Mike, our 14 month old, seemed happy as he kicked and giggled while I buckled him into his stroller.

I had been praying, as hard as I have ever prayed, that I would not have to kill this man. It was a real possibility that I didn't want to happen. I whispered a short prayer just before Mike and I rolled down the driveway towards the street. We made the left turn towards the park just in time to hear the racing engine and screeching of tires as the guy skid to a stop next to us in his truck. He had the window down and screamed that he was fed up and going to kill me right now. As he reached down under his seat, I remember reaching into my pocket for the 38. I had it out of my pocket just as a loud crack rang out. Not a shot, it was the slamming of my neighbor's front door. With that, I saw him throw down to the floorboard whatever was in his right hand and he sped off. I put the gun back in my pocket and turned the stroller back into the driveway, now sweating and shaking all over. Later, my neighbor told me that he had no idea why he went to the door but when he saw what was happening, slamming his door was the only thing this elderly gentleman could think of to do. I don't know if he was Christian but I know God used him that morning and answered my prayer.

Even though I didn't want to, I was totally prepared to kill this man as he threatened us that morning. Just before we finally moved away, having been so angry at the whole situation and at him - I had even considered just doing away with him. I still thank the Lord for forgiving me for those terrible thoughts. We'll not consider here whether, if things had progressed that morning on the street, killing him would have been a sin. I know for a fact that doing so on my own without direct cause would have been murder and that even the consideration of such a terrible thing is a sin. I didn't cause the situation. It wasn't our fault. But I sinned greatly just the same. Never have I ever felt more in need of forgiveness. I later asked the Lord to give me the strength to pray for this man and He swiftly answered that prayer. I have prayed for him many times. The last credible information I had was that he was now a patient in our state mental hospital.

In his letter to the Romans, Paul recounts quotes from early, Old Testament, scriptures that none, Jew or Gentile (non-Jew) are without sin:

> Rom. 3:10-12 *"As it is written: There is no one righteous, not even one; there is no one who understands, no one who seeks God. All have turned away, they have together become worthless; there is no one who does good, not even one"* (Note: *A collection of OT quotations that underscores Paul's charge that both Jews and Gentiles are under the power of sin.)*

The Old Testament book of Leviticus describes the 'sin-offering' required in those times. Since we seldom read or hear of this subject, I have chosen to present whole sections of Chapter Four and it's accompanying notes for you here. There are other scripture books and many verses dealing with atonement sacrifice but this particular text offers a clear explanation and example of what the law required of early believers. The process of atonement for sin was cumbersome and detailed and to carry out the process in error had the gravest of consequences.

> Leviticus 4:1-12 *"The Lord said to Moses, Say to the Israelites: When anyone sins unintentionally and does what is forbidden in any of the Lord's commands*
> —

If the anointed priest sins, bringing guilt on the people, he must bring to the Lord a young bull without defect as a sin offering for the sin he has committed. He is to present the bull at the entrance to the Tent of Meeting before the Lord. He is to lay his hand on its head and slaughter it before the Lord. Then the anointed priest shall take some of the bull's blood and carry it into the Tent of Meeting. He is to dip his finger into the blood and sprinkle some of it seven times before the Lord, in front of the curtain of the sanctuary. [Holy of Holies where God Himself was present for the people] *The priest shall then put some of the blood on the horns of the altar of fragrant incense that is before the Lord in the Tent of Meeting. The rest of the bull's blood he shall pour out at the base of the altar of burnt offering at the entrance to the Tent of Meeting. He shall remove all the fat from the bull of the sin offering – the fat that covers the inner parts or is connected to them, both kidneys with the fat on them near the loins, and the covering of the liver, which he will remove with the kidneys – just as the fat is removed from the ox sacrificed as a fellowship offering. Then the priest shall burn them on the altar of burnt offering. But the hide of the bull and all its flesh, as well as the head and the legs, the inner parts and offal – that is, all the rest of the bull – he must take outside the camp to a place ceremoni-*

> *ally clean where the ashes are thrown, and burn it in a wood fire on the ash heap." (Note: anointed priest- The high priest sins. All high priests sinned except the high priest Jesus Christ. b) on the people- The relationship of the priests to the people was so intimate in Israel (as a nation consecrated to God) that the people became guilty when the priest sinned. 4:4 Three principles of atonement are found in this verse: [1] Substitution {present the bull}, [2] Identification {lay his hand on it's head}, and [3] the death of the substitute {slaughter it})*

See what I mean. A weighty and detailed process indeed. There were four levels of personal sin which were addressed in this way. 1) "the anointed priest," 2) "the whole Israelite community," 3) a "leader," and 4) a "member of the community." That last one would be you and I. The sacrifice process for a "member of the community" wasn't much easier than for the priest:

> Leviticus 4:27- *"If a member of the community sins unintentionally and does what is forbidden in any of the Lord's commands, he is guilty. When he is made aware of the sin he committed, he must bring as his offering for the sin he committed a female goat without defect. He is to lay his hand on the head of the sin offering and slaughter it at the place of the burnt*

offering. Then the priest is to take some of the blood with his finger and put it on the horns of the altar of burnt offering and pour out the rest of the blood at the base of the altar. He shall remove all the fat, just as the fat is removed from the fellowship offering, and the priest shall burn it on the altar as an aroma pleasing to the Lord. In this way the priest will make atonement for him, and he will be forgiven.

Can you just imagine the line outside the temple today? I won't list it all for you here but in chapter five of the same book, there are some other things listed as sinful acts for which atonement was required:

Lev. 5:1 *"If a person sins because he does not speak up when he hears a public charge to testify regarding something he has seen or learned about, he will be held responsible."*

Lev. 5:2 *" Or if a person touches anything ceremonially unclean…even though he is unaware of it, he has become unclean and is guilty."*

Lev 5:3 *"Or if he touches human uncleanness – anything that would make him unclean – even though he is unaware of it, when he learns of it he will be guilty."*

> Lev. 5:4 *"Or if a person thoughtlessly takes an oath to do anything, whether good or evil – in any matter one might carelessly swear about – even though he is unaware of it, in any case when he learns of it he will be guilty."*

I am far from perfect. So are you. So are we all and, to get into Heaven, we absolutely have to be perfect. This is simply a physical impossibility in the tormented world in which we live since the fall into sin. It's humanly impossible. God had to provide a way for us to become – and remain – perfect. We have to remain that way because none but God know the hour of our death. What if death came before our last prayer for forgiveness - and since our last sin? How can we remain forgiven and perfect and, at the same time, still sin? Through Jesus Christ – because of Jesus Christ – and by the Grace of an everlasting Love, God sees us as that new, perfect creation.

The requirement is total perfection in every way. God can tolerate nothing else since He Himself is a perfect being. In Heaven there is total peace and perfection so we can't be there unless we fulfill the requirement to be there. We have to be perfect. Remember Leviticus as you read on. God knew that the early system of payments and atonements wasn't going to work. Every person lived under the heavy weight of their constant thoughts and actions which fell far short of the requirement. They spent all their time figuring out how to make the correct atonement for some sin they had committed.... They weren't free to live. It was nearly impossible for them to do anything constructive for the Lord because of their inborn sinful nature and the process for atonement. Man needed a way to get out from under the weight of his sinful nature and it's eternal consequence.

THE WAY

✥ ✥ ✥

John 11:25,26 Jesus is speaking
"I am the resurrection and the life. He who believes in me will live, even though he dies; and whoever lives and believes in me will never die. Do you believe this?"

✢ ✢ ✢

Sure, you know that Jesus saves. You've heard it a thousand times or more. You've sung those words or similar in hymns over and over. But how does He save us? How can we get from where we are – to where He wants us to be? The Disciples also wanted to know. Jesus said in his own words when asked how to follow where He was going; "I am the way, the truth and the life. No one comes to the Father except through me." (John 14:6) But just what is the 'way'? Well, like He said, He, Jesus, is.

When we read those words, "the way" in different verses, many things can come to mind. Maybe we recall the exact scripture just quoted above. Maybe, to some, those words represent a formula for living (according to "the way"); for others, possibly, a way of thinking (keep a close rein on my thoughts according to "the way"). Look at that verse again and in place of the word 'way', insert either the words payment or sacrifice.

"I am the payment…"

To me, this is a clearer context of that profound verse and a sharper picture of our means of personal salvation - if, that is, we understand why it's necessary to begin with.

After the fall of Adam (mankind) in the Garden of Eden, God established His law for us to live by. The law was a set of rules. However, the law could not save – it only condemned. It was an unyielding set of rules. It was black and white. The law was specific and held specific penalties for various 'sins' against, or breaches of, the law. The only way to get reconciled to God while under the law was to offer certain unblemished sacrifices at an altar dedicated to Him. Nearly all of those sacrifices were animal and involved the spilling of blood – death – as a payment for the transgression involved. The breach of some laws carried the penalty of immediate death for the person or persons involved. That death penalty also meant an eternity void of God, an eternity in hell.

Along with the need to bring living sacrifices in payment for sins was the fact that man had to bring them to the Temple. The sacrifice had to be given to the priest and only this high priest had access to the Altar of the Lord. God, Himself, maintained a presence in this room. So special, so Holy, was this room which contained the altar that the high priest who entered had a rope tied around his body. In case the priest was blemished or unworthy in some unknown way and the Lord struck him dead – his body could be removed from the room without others entering and facing sure and certain death. This method of reckoning for our sins was not easy on anyone involved.

By the time of Moses in early Biblical history, there were some 600 laws that had been introduced under which we were to live or die. There was no way on earth to successfully live – perfectly – under the law. On the mountain when speaking to Moses, God simplified the law into His Ten Commandments. It didn't help. There was simply no way to live without breaking a Commandment and breaking just one, one time without correct payment, meant an eternity in hell after ones death.

Prophets foretold of a Savior coming. This magnificent gift from God which would, *once and for all*, give mankind the means to satisfy the requirements of the law. This gift, this Savior, would be the payment, the sacrifice, required at the altar – forever. Jesus was given to us by God. He was sent here on purpose. His coming was no accident and God's sending Him was no afterthought. From 'the beginning' God knew that He would send Jesus on this perilous and imperative salvation mission to man. A perfect and permanent, once for all, Savior.

> John 3:16 Jesus is speaking *"For God so loved the world that he gave his only begotten son, that whosoever believes in him shall not perish but have eternal life."*

> John 11:25,26 Jesus is speaking *"I am the resurrection and the life. He who believes in me will live, even though he dies; and whoever lives and believes in me will never die. Do you believe this?"*

The fruit of Christ's redemption is not that He merely opened for man the way to reconciliation with God, and that God is now ready and willing to forgive sins, pending certain conditions man must first fulfill. The fruit of Christ's redemption is that Christ actually did effect a reconciliation, that God does no longer impute sins, but has in His heart forgiven all sins to all men. On the part of God reconciliation and the forgiveness of sins is not a mere possibility, but an accomplished fact, an objective reality, which is not affected by the personal attitude of man. [9]

BAPTISM

✣ ✣ ✣

Matthew 28:18-20 Jesus is speaking:

"All authority in heaven and on earth has been given to me. Therefore go and make disciples of all nations, baptizing them in the name of the Father and of the Son and of the Holy Spirit, and teaching them to obey everything I have commanded you. And surely I am with you always, to the very end of the age."

✤ ✤ ✤

Are you baptized? If so, do you remember your baptism? Many are baptized as infants and obviously don't have any memory at all of this most important day. Others are baptized when they become of age, in the eyes of their church. I was baptized when I was eight years old. Although the memories are a bit cloudy now, I remember the event. I don't remember feeling anything odd or any different at all during my baptism. In fact, it felt a little odd to be at the front of the church before all those people. The pastor touched water to my forehead and said the words which make the miracle come to life – "Gary Lewis Johnson, I baptize you in the name of the Father, and of the Son, and the Holy Spirit." That was it. No lightening bolts – no thunder – nothing felt different – but a miracle had just happened. My name had just been added to the Book of Life in Heaven. There has been a lot said and written about baptism, what it is, what it renders to the believer, and so forth. Some of what is being taught I would question.

Baptism was commanded by Jesus himself. The great commission of the Church on earth is to baptize every living person. Other than what Jesus commanded, the "whys" of baptism are long and deeply scriptural. It would take a lot of space to include the whole of baptismal theology in this chapter. However, the core of this sacrament is easy enough to understand and ponder. Christ said we should all be baptized.

> Mat. 28:18-20 *Jesus is speaking "All authority in heaven and on earth has been given to me. Therefore go and make disciples of all nations, baptizing them in the name of the Father and of the Son and of the Holy Spirit, and teaching them to obey everything I have commanded you. And surely I am with you always, to the very end of the age."*

More than meets the eye is contained in the wording of these verses. Christ restates His ultimate authority over all of us and everything in the first seven words. He, Christ, was given all authority by God the Father regarding our eternal destiny. His command to the disciples and, through them, to all the Church (we are the Church, not only the clergy) was to go and baptize "all nations." In those two words, all nations, are included the whole of humanity. The reasoning is that a "nation" is not just men and not just adults or those instructed in the word. Even when Jesus said those words, a nation consisted of every age and sex of human just like today – infant through elder, man and woman. Those old enough to be instructed were taught about The Word first before they were baptized. However, it is very clear that <u>all</u> were to be baptized. When a child or infant was brought for baptism by those who had authority over them, the baptism which occurred effected forgiveness and the presence of the Holy Spirit. That child was immediately, also, brought into the family of Christ (Acts 2:38-39).

> "Infants are to be baptized, because they certainly are included in '<u>all</u> <u>nations</u>.' As little as they can be excluded from the term 'nation,' so little dare we exclude them from Baptism. Also, to infants Christ promises the kingdom of God in Luke 18:15-17."[10]

How we baptize is important only in regards to the words spoken. Christ gave His formula very clearly. We are to baptize "in the name of the Father, and of the Son, and of the Holy Spirit." The person doing the baptism has no power at all. Neither is a special water or any specific amount of water required. The only requirement is that there, indeed, be some water used and that these exact words be spoken as the water is applied. Although there is clear reference to being fully immersed into water during baptisms which occurred in scripture, there are also references to sprinklings of water, as well. Since the water itself carries no power – there is no additional power in full emersion. There is nothing wrong with it either and if one desires the symbolism of this "full" baptism, it is fully beneficial and acceptable. There are contemporary churches, however, which teach that any sort of baptism short of fully dunking the person completely under water is no valid baptism. This is clearly unscriptural by all accounts. Remember, it's not the person or the water which have the saving power but rather the water – in union – with the Word of God. Because of this, even though the Church would rightly prefer that baptisms be performed by ministers – it is perfectly binding and acceptable for any Christian to baptize another in an emergency or where there is the desire to be baptized and no minister is reasonably available to perform that rite.

I was born in early June of 1958 along with my twin brother, Glenn. We were very premature and there weren't the resources which exist today to deal with such emergencies. After just one day, Glenn died. I don't think he was baptized but he may have been by a nurse – this was more common in that time than you might think. Scripture clearly tells us that those who believe and are baptized shall be saved. Christ commanded that we of the Church should be baptized. Because of this, if we have the knowledge that this is commanded by Christ, and do not follow through with being baptized when it is possible to do so, we cannot receive the benefits of Baptism. However, it is only lack of belief which damns (Mark 16:15-16). Where there is no opportunity to be baptized or no knowledge that this rite exists – we must defer to the majesty and mercy of God. We have the promise of Christ in His own words telling us that whoever believes in Him shall not perish. So what of my infant brother who could not hear the Word and whom I believe was not baptized? I can only offer him, and all others like him, to an infinitely graceful and loving God. I believe that, lacking specific words of explanation in the scriptures, we have to leave them in the hands and in the care of our loving God. And you know what – that's a pretty good place to be! I take comfort in the fact that the Bible tells us all God wants us to know…*it does not tell us all that there is to know.* We are told in the Gospels that Christ worked miracles which were not described to us in those writings. We know that mans understanding of things is laughable compared to the wisdom and mercy of God. I am fully content to leave Glenn in the hands of God until I get there…. I am confident he'll be there to greet me!

WHAT ABOUT SPECIFIC SINS?

✣ ✣ ✣

Ephesians 2:8-10

"For it is by grace you have been saved, through faith – and this not from yourselves, it is the gift of God – not by works, so that no one can boast. For we are God's workmanship…"

✥ ✥ ✥

If there is anything in this current day and age which has driven a wedge between Christians it is the subject of "specific sin." You won't find that term anywhere in the Bible and yet nothing has been more confusing to Christians. No tool of Satan has been more useful to him than the doubt created by those accusing others over their sins. Even more, the doubt we create within ourselves. The worry of whether something we've done will keep us from being saved or the question of if our salvation is really sure. Unfortunately, the contemporary church has given credence to the notion that holiness, the need to be holy, is almost equal to the need to be saved. When in fact, holiness and the sanctified life which springs from it, only comes as a result of salvation.

> Eph 2:8-10 *"For it is by grace you have been saved, through faith – and this not from yourselves, it is the*

gift of God – not by works, so that no one can boast. For we are God's workmanship..."

We all sin. The Greek word for sin in the New Testament is "hamartia" and is defined as "missing the mark"[11] of God's righteousness. There is no living person who doesn't sin. Although the Bible certainly brings out certain sinful actions and behaviors that are reprehensible to the Lord, none of them is listed as a sin which is beyond forgiveness - except one which we will discuss later. For now, let's look at things like murder, homosexuality, and adultery which are typically regarded as some of the "worst" sins. By Biblical definition, anything which is contrary to the Will of our Perfect God is sin. Any thought, any action, however large or small, if it is wrong is a sin - any sin is damming and there is no one sin greater than another. In the light of John 3:16, I can find no place in scripture which defines that any type of sin is 'worse' than another – **with regard to forgiveness and salvation.** It just isn't there, anywhere. Sin is sin. Nobody is immune. All men, women, and children sin. There is a lot of hate generated today by people who say they are Christians and yet want to declare that others aren't because of some action or lifestyle. Now, please let me be clear, sin is sin. If one participates in these socially acceptable behaviors such as homosexuality, browsing pornographic activity, and the like – it's still sin, a violation of God's will. I don't say this of my own accord but rather repeat it from the Bible. And yet, there are different consequences for "anti-social" behaviors here on earth. However, in the eyes of God, hatred is the same as murder; lust is the same as adultery, but both have very different consequences here in society and in the eyes of the State. Every single sin ever to be committed – ever - has already – 2007 years ago - been forgiven by the death and resurrection of our Lord Jesus at the Cross. Many learned men and women try to spin Bible verses into saying something that they do not say about the severity of sin. Remember two of the verses I mentioned so far:

"My yoke is easy and my burden is light"

"...whoever believes in him shall not perish but have eternal life"

That one section of John 3:16 (as quoted above), should be the bedrock of our conviction and assurance of salvation. I believe that if any pastor, church, denomination or man teach that any sort of 'continual sin' is an *automatic* path to damnation – they are in violation of scripture! Those who teach, especially, that homosexuality is, in effect, turning against God because it is unnatural – and so – is the same as committing that one unforgivable sin – don't understand scripture. The Apostle Paul does state in Galatians that there are sins which jeopardize our relationship with God but *only* if there is no repentance in <u>this life</u>.

Gal 5:19-21 *"The acts of the sinful nature are obvious: sexual immorality, impurity and debauchery; idolatry and witchcraft; hatred, discord, jealousy, fits of rage, selfish ambition, dissensions, factions and envy; drunkenness, orgies and the like. I warn you, as I did before, that those who <u>live</u> [continually and consciously without remorse] like this will not inherit the kingdom of God."* Emphasis added.

As important as it is, I haven't yet mentioned repentance on purpose because repentance is a personal thing. Only we know if we are sorry or regret any sin we have committed. Moreover, our outward actions don't necessarily tell others whether we actually have repented. No person and no church has the right to judge whether I am repentant of my sins based on my actions even though our actions should reflect our faith. Also, the fact that in any way I forget to repent of a sin does not mean that I cannot be forgiven of that sin. It also doesn't necessarily mean that I am not sorry that I do it. Nobody knows but me – and God! Let me take a moment and list some other sins which we might daily commit and which are against the will of God:

Cheating on taxes	Cheating of any type
Drinking to excess	Speeding
Breaking any civil law	Cursing
Spending time on the internet at work	Surfing the net for porn
Anti-Semitism or bigotry	Stealing anything at all – even paperclips
Being judgmental of others	Lying
Premarital sex of any type	Spousal abuse
Elder abuse	Not being willing to work
Little white lies	

This list could go on and on. No one is exempt. Any single or continual sinful action is a perversion of God's will and brings us under His Devine Judgment! The only thing that matters is our prayers to God about the forgiveness of our sin and no man on earth knows when or what those are!

I've given this a lot of prayerful thought. You see, homosexuality exists in my own family. Listening to many of the church leaders of my time, led me to believe that anyone homosexual was beyond salvation and eternally dammed. I fought with this terrible lie for years. I don't really know whether homosexuality is a result of genetics or life choice. It doesn't matter – it's sinful. Alcohol addiction, for instance, has been statistically shown to be genetically passed, inherited. It's still sinful even if those afflicted can't help it. But even so, this has no bearing on whether these brothers and sisters are saved or not. None! If you are a church leader or Christian walking with me through this and are of the opinion that all homosexuals are dammed, you're simply wrong. Yes, it is a perversion according to Romans 1:27, but not beyond repentance and forgiveness. Transgression of specific sin is no guide for our condemnation – or not – relative to our salvation. That judgment belongs only to God.

We should repent of our sins. However, repentance is a subject of which all Christians ought be cautious to bring up in conversations with others. To keep to the subject, let me just say, **our salvation is not dependent on our daily repentance**. You see, it can't be that way. We sin nearly every minute or hour of our life in one way or another. The Bible tells us that our very nature itself is sinful. Since we don't know when the Lord may call us to be with Him, how would we ever be able to keep track of when we last repented. What about sins we commit of which we are unaware. Those exist you know. In anger or otherwise, we often commit sins of which we have no recollection. This being the case, we don't know to ask for forgiveness for them. So, I will say it again, our salvation has nothing at all to do with how often we repent – or – what we repent of at any given time. Specific sin has no bearing at all on if we are saved. What does matter is <u>whether we admit that we are sinful and confess that sinful-</u>

ness. God already knows everything we think, have done, or will do in our life. It's not up to Him to ask – it's up to us to admit. He makes this very clear in His Word.

The Bible mentions only one sin which is unforgivable. If you commit this sin, you won't be asking for forgiveness anyway. The one unforgivable sin is the total, abject, rejection of God. Total disbelief that He even exists or ever has existed. What is total rejection? An example might be whether you believe the moon is made of cheese. Do you believe that? Absolutely not, and nobody could convince you otherwise. More than that, if anybody did try to convince you that the moon was made of cheese – you would think that they themselves were twisted and in need of help. Abject rejection of God is rejection to the point that you believe in Him as much as you believe that the moon is made of cheese – it might also be believing that ones sin is so great that God could not forgive it. That, my friends, is as close as I can come to describing how far a Christian would need to fall –in belief - to commit this one unforgivable sin. That's pretty far! Anything above that level is not that level and there's hope! There is nothing in the Bible which says that committing any sin – for any length of time – is such a perversion as to be equal to committing this one unforgivable sin. If anyone has inferred this, as far as I can understand Scripture, they were wrong. If that reasoning were true, then anyone who commits any sin over and over would have to be branded the same way and there are plenty of

Christians who do just that - in fact - all of us do. I have heard church leaders on the radio teach that living a homosexual life is akin to "anti-God" and, therefore, the same as committing this unforgivable sin of abject rejection. They could not be further from the truth and have, themselves, twisted God's Word. Again, they are right in pointing out the obvious sin of homosexuality. Unmarried sex is just as much a sin if you are heterosexual. Let me say it this way - if we're gay, if we're heterosexual and having sex outside of marriage, if we're sinning in any other consistent manner of which we are aware - our "lifestyle" is sinful and we should be asking forgiveness daily, if possible. Moreover, like any Christian who is struggling with sin of which they are aware, we should honestly be looking for ways to leave that sin behind. But this should be the end of the discussion. The issue is between ourselves and the Lord – not one another. You know where you stand and He certainly does. Look, any sin in our life is no different and all of us – every one of us no matter how much better than "they" we may think we are – are every bit as much depraved and deluded. The truth is, without Grace – we would all be totally lost forever and on our way to hell when we die. Christ had an admonishment for those who would judge others:

> Luke 6:41 Jesus is speaking *"Why do you look at the speck of sawdust in your brother's eye and pay no attention to the plank in your own eye?"*

THAT GRACE THING – IT'S A BIG THING

✥ ✥ ✥

2 Corinthians 11:7-9,

"...there was given me a thorn in my flesh, a messenger of Satan, to torment me. Three times I pleaded with the Lord to take it away from me. But he said to me, 'My grace is sufficient for you, for my power is made perfect in weakness.'"

✜ ✜ ✜

In his letter to the Corinthians, The Apostle Paul talks with God about a "thorn." Read the following verse and particularly notice God's answer:

> 2 Cor. 11:7-9, *"...there was given me a thorn in my flesh, a messenger of Satan, to torment me. Three times I pleaded with the Lord to take it away from me. But he said to me, 'My grace is sufficient for you, for my power is made perfect in weakness.'"*

"My Grace is sufficient for you." I believe God was, in effect, saying to Paul and through Paul to all of us:

GOD: [You are sinful, I know this and have always known this. I know you can't stop sinning and never will. Quit worrying about it and let Me use you. I'm a merciful God and my Son's death and resurrection paid for your sins

– all of them. I don't even remember them anymore.] (See Jeremiah 31:34)

We aren't told what that 'thorn' was. There is speculation among scholars that it was some sort of moral, ethical, or physical infirmity that caused Paul anguish. Whatever it was, it was causing him to suffer in a way he had difficulty accepting and he wanted rid of the problem. Sometimes, we can't bear the anguish in our own lives. Oh that it wasn't so. Paul knew very well that he couldn't stop the infirmity. He knew he couldn't be whole but, at the same time, he despised his infirmity. There is a section of his letter to the Romans which deals exactly with this truth. We can sense the frustration in his writing:

Romans 7:15-24 *"I do not understand what I do. For what I want to do – I do not do – but [rather] what I hate to do. And if I do what I do not want to do, I agree that the law is good* [in pointing it out to me]. *As it is, it is no longer I myself who do it [new creation] but it is <u>sin living within me</u>. I know that nothing good lives in me, that is, in my sinful nature. For I have the desire to do what is good, but I cannot carry it out. For what I do is not the good I want to do; no, the evil I do not want to do – this I keep on doing. Now if I do what I do not want to do, it is no longer I who do it, but it is sin living in me that does it. So I* *find this law at work: When I want to do good, evil is right there with me. For in my inner being I delight in God's law; but I see another law at work in the members of my body, waging war against the law of my mind and making me a prisoner of the law of sin at work within my members. What a wretched man I am! Who will rescue me from this body of death?"* Emphasis added.

As frustrated as he was however, Paul came to a very important conclusion. His words at the end of the verse are the explanation of how we are sinful - yes - and, at the same time, redeemed in the eyes of the Lord. Our sinful nature, in God's eyes, has been separated from the Godly creation we become anew through redemption. Without God's saving Grace we would all be doomed and yet we forget what that Grace means for us.

Grace is freely given. We can't buy it and don't deserve it. When Jesus died on the cross, he was making the total sacrificial payment – at that very moment – for each and every sin yet committed or ever to be committed by any person ever to be born. Whatever you may have been involved in so far in your life, it is no surprise to the Lord. He isn't sitting up on His throne with a perplexed look on his face and saying, "Gee, I didn't know you were going to do that!" No, he saw it all way back in the very beginning of time and when Jesus died, He paid for our sins – all of them – in advance - every single one. In reality, we are free to do anything we want. Paul knew this and, so, in his first letter to the Corinthians in a section dealing with sexual immorality he touched on the subject:

> 1 Cor. 6:12 *"Everything is permissible for me – but not everything is beneficial. Everything is permissible for me – but I will not be mastered by anything."*

Any sinful thing we do has been forgiven already. **HOWEVER** and as Paul said, this does not mean that we should take advantage of God and trample on the tremendous gift of Grace. If we realize what we have been given, we should want to do the opposite whenever possible! Grace has some bit of risk for us as it is easy to take advantage of the all-encompassing nature of that gift. There is, however, a fine line. Only God knows how far His Grace is available to any man. To suggest that any action, or lack of action, might not be covered by His Grace is getting into dangerous, shark infested, waters. We must be very cautious if we follow in this direction. Remember, every single sinful anything was covered by the death and resurrection of Christ. There is nothing that wasn't foreseen or that may have been missed. Forgiveness is a fact for all sins of man. So, the question then becomes, who of us can really say that we are forgiven? That's what the argument seems to boil down to for some

Christians. They may argue that you and I don't have the right, because of this or that, to claim our forgiveness won on the Cross. In his book, "What's So Amazing About Grace?", author Philip Yancey quotes a theologian and preacher named Martin Lloyd-Jones. He writes:

> "There is thus clearly a sense in which the message of "justification by faith only" can be dangerous, and likewise with the message that salvation is entirely of grace..."

> "I would say to all preachers: If your preaching of salvation has not been misunderstood in that way, then you had better examine your sermons again, and you had better make sure that you really are preaching the salvation that is offered in the New Testament to the ungodly, to the sinner, to those who are enemies of God. There is this kind of dangerous element about the true presentation of the doctrine of salvation."[12]

The father of all protestant churches, Dr. Martin Luther, went even further. Of the concept of Grace and sins he wrote:

> In a letter from Luther to his friend Melanchthon, "If you are a preacher of grace, do not preach a fictitious,

but a true, grace; and if the grace is true, carry a true, and not a fictitious sin. Be a sinner and sin vigorously...It is sufficient that we recognize through the wealth of God's glory, the Lamb who bears the sin of the world; from this, sin does not sever us, even if thousands of times in one day we should fornicate or murder."[13]

The price Christ paid was so huge and so perfect that God tells us He has removed our sin from us and remembers our sin no longer. The Psalmist, David, also said,

Psalm 103:11,12 *"For as high as the heavens are above the earth, so great is his love for those who fear him; as far as the East is from the West, so far has he removed our transgressions from us."*

Isa. 43:25 *"I, even I, am he who blots out your transgressions, for my own sake, and remembers your sins no more."*

Heb. 8:12 *"For I will forgive their wickedness and will remember their sins no more."*

We never know where life will lead. Friends and family enter or pass through our life at different times and the world goes round seemingly without end. Things happen which shape our feelings and perceptions. Sometimes, we bring the world down on our shoulders as a result of our own actions. At other times, through no fault of our own, the same thing can happen and we can loose touch with the Lord and others who care about us. Both were the case with my Uncle Lewis. Unckie, as we called him, was an ex-navy radio operator from the Korean War era. To say that he had lived up to the sailor stereotype would be a big understatement from what I've heard about him over the years. However rough his edges may have been, years wore them smooth and by the time I came into his life – he was just Unckie. A tall guy with a good singing voice and I loved him deeply.

He took my brother and I fishing one time with a group of men. I think I was about ten years old. Doing what I shouldn't have been doing, I slipped down the bank and into the water of the river where we were camped. I remember it was a steep slope and I could not touch bottom. It was night-time and the only person around was my younger brother Mike. He had a really worried look on his face as he stared down at me while I was grasping the weeds on the edge of the bank. Thank goodness Mike was doing what he shouldn't have been doing in leaving the camp with me. There was a current, but not too swift, and I remember briefly thinking that I might be able to swim to some other area along the bank where I could get out. Instead, I told Mike to run and get Unckie. He ran off screaming into the darkness and in just a few seconds, I could hear Uncle Lewis' heavy footsteps coming through the woods. With one swift movement, he reached down and pulled me out of the water by my one arm. We'll never know for sure but he probably saved my life because ten year olds swimming in rivers at night don't usually survive. He didn't get angry. He just put me by the fire so I could warm up. Now that I think of it, this was the only time Unckie took us fishing.

A few years later when I was in Junior High, Lewis was in a bad car accident and suffered a terrible head injury. He recovered to the extent possible with the knowledge available in the early 1970's. As happens so often with such an injury, he was just never the same. Years went by, and after loosing his wife to cancer, he began to drink again. Life, and drinking, took it's toll and he lost his job and pretty much everything he had left. In the end, he was living in a government subsidized little house and drinking every penny he had to his name. My dad called one day and asked if I could come and help him with Lewis. I didn't realize how bad off he was and I was shocked when we arrived, even though dad had warned me what to expect. We found him naked, sitting in an old chair covered in his own waste, and unable to move much. I can still see him there. His body was swollen and sick from the toxic effects of so much alcohol. I helped dad pick him up. Together, we wrapped him in a blanket, placed him in the car and took him to the hospital. After several trips to the hospital in the coming weeks, Lewis finally decided that he wasn't going to the hospital any more. We were in the ER one night when he made this decision by pulling out his IV's and catheter and shouting a cursing plea to be taken home. His system was so toxic due to kidney failure that the doctors assured him if he left the ER, he would be dead by weeks end. They were right.

We took him home and set up a schedule to be with him 'round the clock. That first evening our little family was all there with him; Diane and I, my dad and his wife Shirley, my brother, and my Grandma Sadie. I was on the bed beside Lewis talking with him about things and the thought came to me to ask him if he might like to partake of the Lord's Supper. I'm sure it was the Lord's idea. Lewis said "no" and I was disappointed. A bit later, dad came and got me saying that Lewis wanted to see me. When I sat down beside him he said, "Gary Lewis, I want to." He hadn't been in a church in years and I realized that I had offered something that there was no clergy to call on to give. Even though there might have been a minister in the little town of Willis, Tx who would have come, we weren't sure at all how much time Unckie had left. So, Mike and I went to the store and purchased a loaf of uncut bread and a bottle of red wine. With our family in the small room as witness and with my brother to assist, I asked Lewis the same questions that I remember our Pastor asking so many times as Baptisms were performed. "Do you believe that Jesus Christ is true God and that He died and rose again from the grave for your sins?" "Do you renounce the devil in all his works and all his ways?" After Lewis had, with a weak and raspy voice, reconfirmed his belief in Christ and renounced the devil, we broke the bread and poured wine into a small plastic cup. As I read the words of institution from the Bible, Lewis shared in the blessing of the Lord's Supper. A few days later, while sitting by his side listening to the terrible crackling and wheezing that comes when death is near, I remember bending down to his ear and telling him, "Unckie, just ask Jesus to help you and He will." He died a few hours later that night.

Uncle Lewis loved country music. A well known song writer and singer named Don Williams wrote a song titled "I Believe in You." In that song is the lyric: "I don't believe that Heaven waits for only those who congregate." I love that simple little line because it's so true. As I spoke at his funeral, it was a great comfort to tell those who only saw the outward Lewis of recent months, that he, indeed, was a saved man. Lewis is a man now rid of his worldly, filthy, body having traded that wretched tent for his unblemished garment reserved for those who rest with Jesus – by Grace alone.

We sin. Yes, God knows that we sin every day and only He knows how depraved we really are and how far we may sink in this life. However, in the end, God has already cleared the ledger. This is a fact. There is no 'big' sin which wasn't covered by Christ and there is no 'little' sin which wasn't paid for as well on that cross. There is no human life too far gone for God to rescue. Reread John 3:16 if you feel you, or anyone you know, are beyond His forgiveness. You aren't beyond it! It has already happened! You *already have* forgiveness from God. Please - forgive yourself as well - and remember that others have His forgiveness too.

JUDGEMENT AND REWARD VS. SALVATION

✣ ✣ ✣

Matthew 6:19,20

"Do not store up for yourselves treasures on earth, where moth and rust destroy, and where thieves break in and steal. But store up for yourselves treasurers in Heaven…"

✤ ✤ ✤

A good bit of confusion in our Christian lives, I believe, stems out of a misunderstanding of the difference between - our salvation – which gets us to Heaven and - our reward - once we get to Heaven. It is critical to understand the difference. While our salvation is won by Christ and our sin-laden lives do not negate the Grace of God, our actions in this life do have an effect on our life hereafter. They add-to or diminish our rewards in Heaven. Have you ever considered that difference before? Perhaps not. Not knowing this fact can create a big haze in our mind's picture of salvation.

> Mat. 6:18 *"...and your Father, who sees what is done in secret, will reward you."*

> Mat. 6:19,20 *"Do not store up for yourselves treasures on earth, where moth and rust destroy, and*

where thieves break in and steal. But store up for yourselves treasurers in Heaven..."

There are several references to our reward, treasures, etc. in the Bible. Some of them, indeed, do relate to our life journey towards salvation, but not all. There is one very important biblical insight in Paul's first letter to the Corinthians. This verse describes very clearly that there is, and will be, a difference for us when God judges our works – not our salvation – on the last day.

1 Cor. 3:14,15 *"If what he has built survives, he will receive his reward. If it is burned up, he will suffer loss; he himself will be saved, but only as one escaping through the flames."*

Paul mentions two separate events in this verse. First, that if a man's actions [work] do not hold up under God's test he – the man – will suffer "loss." Second, that this same man will be "saved." What is it that we could suffer loss of on the day of judgment? Heavenly treasures. God watches our actions and knows our heart and thoughts. He especially likes it when we do something for Him in secret or, at least, in a manner such that we are not looking for recognition for doing it. The scripture points out that when we do these sort of things – because of our love for God and what He has given to us – He sees and remembers and adds treasure to our name in Heaven.

> Mat. 5:12 *Jesus is speaking, "Rejoice and be glad, because great is your reward in heaven…"*

Christ certainly could have said, great is your 'salvation' in Heaven – but that's not the word He chose. He said, "Great is your <u>reward</u>!"

The word judgment in our present society has negative connotations. If you are being judged, then you must have done something wrong or at least there is enough evidence that you have such that society feels the need to conduct a trial. We go before a judge because of a speeding ticket, family law issue like divorce, we are involved in a lawsuit, etc. None of that is fun or pleasurable. However, the judgment coming on the "last day" will not necessarily be what we, as believers, have understood. Think of it this way. There are times when the judge says something like, "there is no basis for this suit or accusation – case dismissed." For believers, the trial won't even get that far. Our trial has already happened. We were guilty but someone else paid our debt – Christ. As such, God only sees us as clean and redeemed. His judgment will not be whether or not we deserve to be saved! Our salvation doesn't get decided on the last day! The things being judged – for saved believers - are the good works done while in this life.

None of our bad or sinful actions will be mentioned – none brought up for view. (Jeremiah 31:34b) Only those things done as good for the glory of God. For those things, God has been stacking up a reward for us. At the moment of *our* judgment, God will present to us His reward based on His judging of our works along the way. All men will render an account for their actions. (Mat. 12:36) Yes, but we won't be seen as *sinful men* we will be seen as sanctified, redeemed, unblemished children of God. Some teach that God will want to know why we did not do better than we did with what He gave us to work with. Not doing better than doing perfectly denotes sin and, as we have already seen, sin was forgiven. There is no spiritual value in suggesting that God, on the one hand, says He has totally forgiven us and sees our failures no more – and then on the other hand – suggesting that on the last day He will call us on the carpet for those same failures. He will, however, recall with us the good we did do for His sake. Our Salvation is by Grace (Eph 2:8-9) but our Judgment is according to works. (Rev 20:12)(Rev 22:12)

For the believers the sentence of condemnation, which under the Law they had deserved by their sins, is suspended and changed into a sentence of pardon and justification, because by faith they have appropriated to themselves the saving merits of Christ. Their sins are not investigated and published; they are not even mentioned. The Judge does not look at the rags of their sins, but sees only the perfect garment of righteousness, which he offered them in the Gospel, and which they put on by faith.[14]

THE QUESTION – THE ANSWER

✣ ✣ ✣

John 10:27-30 Jesus is speaking

"My sheep listen to my voice; I know them, and they follow me. I give them eternal life, and they shall never perish; no one can snatch them out of my hand. My Father, who has given them to me, is greater than all; no one can snatch them out of my Father's hand. I and the Father are one."

✣ ✣ ✣

Without Grace, we have nothing. Generations have now passed away under the veil of sin who have all been the recipients of Grace. If the question is: Am I saved? The answer is: you and God are the only ones who know and don't ever let anyone ever try to convince you otherwise. Have you been baptized? The answer to this, I hope, is yes. If you know that you aren't baptized or can't find out, please – please – contact a friend or your nearest church and tell them you want to be baptized. Do you believe that Jesus Christ actually lived, died and rose again? Is the answer yes? If so, praise God – you're saved! It's just that simple. You can believe in Him and what he did and still be unclear or wonder about a lot of other things in your Christian life! If you were baptized and if you believe in Jesus – you're saved! You have to "believe not" to be damned – totally believe not. (Mk 15:16)

Some are blessed such that they have no fear at all and are totally sure of their place in Heaven. My grandma Sadie was such a person. Grandma was born in Tennessee and raised in central Arkansas. At the very best, her family was dirt poor. She also had a very strict upbringing in the Church of Christ. I think this must have given her the foundation to become the person I knew and loved. Grandma used to tell us that she loved to play basketball. I could never imagine it myself but she recalled being asked to play as center on the girls basketball team in her school. Her mom, however, did not like that the girls wore those "little shorts" and so grandma wasn't allowed to play. Sadie had a spark of life that I rarely see in people today but she certainly had her ups and downs. She was married three times with one of the marriages being very abusive. She had simple ways and saw life through the wisdom that comes with lots of experience and hard knocks. She loved her family deeply and we were her most cherished treasure.

Grandma lived a hard life but, she would certainly say, it was a good one in so many ways. If anything stands out in my memory of her it would be her deep convictions and love of the Lord. Of the many times I would spend the night with her, it would have been uncommon not to see her reading her Bible before we went to bed. I have her Bible now. It is well worn, written in, and shows the use of one who loved His teachings. As many do, towards the end of her life, grandma began to struggle with illness. We once had entered her into a hospice program because she simply could not, or would not, eat. One morning I was at my dad's house. We were to tell her that morning that the doctors had no hope of her survival. A hard thing for anyone to contemplate saying to someone so deeply loved as grandma. Dad let me tell her. When I did, she asked what she needed to do to "stay here." I said, "grandma, you need to eat." "Well, then get me into the kitchen and I'll eat." We have no idea why, on this particular morning, she made that turn. But eat she did in ever increasing amounts and she was a continuing light in our lives for several more years. I still believe that the Lord let her stay just a while longer so my dad – all of us – could adjust our minds and souls to the reality of living on without her.

As I compare the two - my Uncle Lewis died a "hard" death, if that can be said. It was not pleasant for him or for those of us with him in those final hours. It had the marks of one tormented and a body sick from abuse. I had left his house a few hours before he passed but I know it wasn't a peaceful passing. With grandma, it was totally different. My dad, his wife Shirley and I had been with her constantly for several days since the stroke. She was there in mind but could not talk or respond in any real way other than to squeeze our hand when we spoke to her. We sat and read to her from her Bible and told stories about what we remembered fondly of our life with her. At times, even though her mouth was tilted and warped from the damaged nerves, we could still make out a faint smile and she would give a long squeeze to let us know that she too remembered. We were with her when God called - the three of us. It was an honor and a blessing. It was peaceful. I cannot say, and maybe shouldn't imply in any way, that her faith made any difference at all in the manner of her death. I guess, maybe, it was that we had several days of reading scriptures and retelling happy memories that made the difference. Holding her hand as her heart beat it's last is a memory I hope I keep forever. More than that, I can't wait to see her again!

Grandma kept a close rein on her thoughts and actions. She knew of Grace but also knew of the work of Satan. Some Christians are taught "once saved – always saved." Nope, that's not what the Bible says. We have a choice. We have the ability to reject His grace and mock His forgiveness. We can close the account. Scripture tells us that God has given His chosen ones to Jesus and, once given, nothing can wrench them from Jesus' grasp. True enough. However, read that verse closely:

> John 10:27-30 *"My sheep listen to my voice; I know them, and they follow me. I give them eternal life, and they shall never perish; no one can snatch them out of my hand. My Father, who has given them to*

me, is greater than all; no one can snatch them out of my Father's hand. I and the Father are one."

The key is, only an **all-knowing** God knows, through the end of time, **whom** those chosen ones will be – we men do not know and certainly shouldn't guess. All humans have life choices and only God now knows the ones who will persevere in their belief or which ones He will bring into the fold before their final breath. We shouldn't take our gift for granted! We should not live like pagans under the protection of Grace. If you have read this far and finally come to realize that you are, in fact, saved from eternal life in a terrible hell – then please stop right now and thank the Lord for that tremendous gift!

Do you have to show your gratitude for salvation? No. Why in the world would you not? If you have the faith and belief the size of a mustard seed (very small thing indeed) then Jesus himself said you have all it takes to work miracles in the lives of others! Helping others is the best "thank you" we can offer to God. There are a lot of "intellectual Christians" in the world and God doesn't like that very much. Armchair Christians are discussed in a fairly dim light in the book of James. Long story short, when we know we are saved by the suffering and death of Christ Jesus and just sit on that knowledge safe in our little world – that's not a good thing.

(James 4:17) When the disciples asked Him which was the most important commandment, Christ replied:

> Mat. 22:37-40 *"Love the Lord your God with all your heart and with all your soul and with all your mind. This is the first and greatest commandment. And the second is like it: Love your neighbor as yourself. All the Law and the Prophets hang on these two commandments."*

I believe He was probably thinking to himself – "If you can just do that – I've taken care of the rest." When we love something, it usually shows in some way in the course of our daily living. Christ gave us this gift so that we didn't have to spend our life in fear of Him and our eventual judgment. As flawed as we still are, we're free to live. Do that. **Live.**

I have kept a prayer journal off and on for years. This is an amazing way to see how God has responded with his Grace and Love in our lives. It's a little odd feeling to start – kinda like keeping tabs on God. Honestly, it's one of the most uplifting things I've ever done to prove to myself how active God really was in my life. Try it for yourself. Any kind of little notebook will do. To make it easy, I've included 10 pages in the back of this book for you to use. Keep a prayer journal for a couple of weeks. Then, after some time, go back and review your prayers and see how those issues have resolved – or not. If not, it's a good way to let yourself know to keep praying for that person or issue. If so, wonder at how God was involved and answered your prayers. If you do this, after a while, you'll find yourself "looking" for His answers to prayers – and that's exactly what He wants us to do!

I can't tell you what to do now that you know you're saved. Maybe you are old or bedridden or very ill. Maybe you feel that there is nothing left for you to do. Maybe you've never done anything before, ever, for the Lord and don't know what to do or where to begin. The Lord works in amazing and strange but wonderful ways. Remember my neighbor who slammed his front door? The little things we do in life can have a very large effect on the people whom the Lord leads across our path. Pray to Him. Ask Him to give you an answer. I promise you, this is a prayer He will answer in a way you will understand. Be sensitive to Him - expect and be open to His answer. God doesn't expect the whole world of you. What He does expect is honesty with yourself – after all, you can't lie to Him. Search your thoughts. If you believe in Him, ask for His help in what to do about it all. Countless times, in my own life, the Lord has led me to someone, or led them across my path, where I had a chance to be of some help or give some simple word of encouragement in His name.

Just Add Nothing

Above all else, as you continue to ponder your salvation and future life with Him in Heaven and as you think of others – remember – He did it all at Calvary on the cross. He did it for YOU! He did it for everyone.

Believe in Him and — Just add nothing!

ENDNOTES

✣ ✣ ✣

1. Koehler, E. W. A.,(1952), *A Summary of Christian Doctrine*. St. Louis, MO: Concordia Publishing House, p. 2, 1997 Wesley, C. (1990). *Evidence That Demands a Verdict*, McDowell
2. *Who Wrote The Bible?*, www.AllAboutTruth.org, 2002-2007
3. *Who Wrote The Bible?*, www.AllAboutTruth.org, 2002-2007
4. *Who Wrote The Bible?*, www.AllAboutTruth.org, 2002-2007
5. *Who Wrote The Bible?*, www.AllAboutTruth.org, 2002-2007
6. *Who Wrote The Bible?*, www.AllAboutTruth.org, 2002-2007
7. *Who Wrote The Bible?*, www.AllAboutTruth.org, 2002-2007

8. Koehler, *A Summary of Christian Doctrine*, p. 146 10. 11. 12. 13.
9.
10. Koehler, *A Summary of Christian Doctrine*, p. 206-207
11 Thayer and Smith. "Greek Lexicon entry for Hamartia". "The New Testament Greek Lexicon". <http://www.searchgodsword.org/lex/grk/view.cgi?number=266>
12 Yancey, *What's So Amazing About Grace?*, p. 178
13 Yancey, *What's So Amazing About Grace?*, p. 184
14 Koehler, *A Summary of Christian Doctrine*, p. 306

PRAYERS TO MY FATHER

✠ ✠ ✠

PRAYERS TO MY FATHER

✢ ✢ ✢

PRAYERS TO MY FATHER

✣ ✣ ✣

PRAYERS TO MY FATHER

✤ ✤ ✤

PRAYERS TO MY FATHER

✣ ✣ ✣

PRAYERS TO MY FATHER

✣ ✣ ✣

PRAYERS TO MY FATHER

✣ ✣ ✣

PRAYERS TO MY FATHER

✣ ✣ ✣

PRAYERS TO MY FATHER

✣ ✣ ✣

PRAYERS TO MY FATHER

✣ ✣ ✣

PRAYERS TO MY FATHER

✣ ✣ ✣

PRAYERS TO MY FATHER

✠ ✠ ✠

PRAYERS TO MY FATHER

✤ ✤ ✤

Printed in the United States
80477LV00003B/16